The Alamo

by Michael Burgan

Content Adviser: Professor Sherry L. Field,
Department of Social Science Education, College of Education,
The University of Georgia

Reading Adviser: Dr. Linda D. Labbo,
Department of Reading Education, College of Education,
The University of Georgia

COMPASS POINT BOOKS

Minneapolis, Minnesota

Compass Point Books
3722 West 50th Street, #115
Minneapolis, MN 55410

Visit Compass Point Books on the Internet at *www.compasspointbooks.com* or e-mail your request
to *custserv@compasspointbooks.com*

Editors: E. Russell Primm and Emily J. Dolbear
Photo Researcher: Svetlana Zhurkina
Photo Selector: Linda S. Koutris
Designer: Bradfordesign, Inc.

Library of Congress Cataloging-in-Publication Data

Burgan, Michael.
   The Alamo / by Michael Burgan.
     p. cm. —   (We the people)
   Includes bibliographical references and index.
   ISBN 0-7565-0097-4 (lib. bdg.)
     1. Alamo (San Antonio, Tex.)—Siege, 1836—Juvenile literature. [1. Alamo (San Antonio,
Tex.)—Siege, 1836. 2. Texas—History—Revolution, 1835–1836.] I. Title. II. We the people
(Compass Point Books)
   F390 .B9 2001
   976.4'03—dc21   00-011005

TABLE OF CONTENTS

TROUBLE LOOMS

Colonel William B. Travis scanned the flat Texas countryside. He knew trouble was close. Mexican troops had just crossed the Rio Grande. Now, on February 23, 1836, they were entering the town of San Antonio. Travis and

Colonel William B. Travis

others were defending the Alamo, a small fort just north of town. The Mexicans had come to attack Travis and his soldiers.

Many of the people inside the Alamo were Texians—Americans living in Texas. Texas was then part of Mexico. Others in the fort included

4

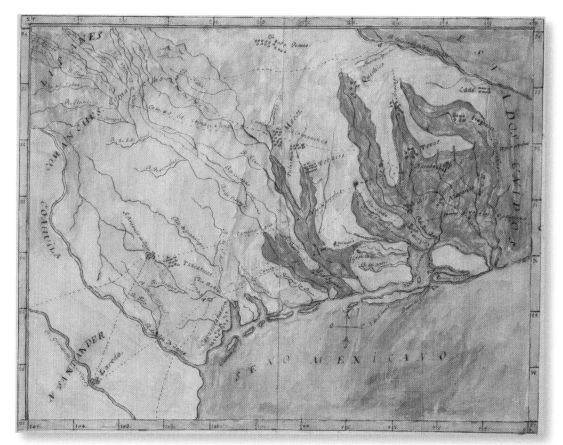

A map showing Texas as a part of Mexico

Tejanos—native Mexicans living in Texas. Some American citizens and a few African-American slaves also lived there. They had fled to the Alamo for safety as the Mexican troops approached San Antonio.

5

*General Antonio
López de Santa Anna*

The Mexican leader was General Antonio López de Santa Anna. He was also the president of Mexico. Santa Anna was ambitious, cunning, and brutal. He once said, "Man is nothing; power is everything." Santa Anna was also a **dictator.** The Texians rebelled against his rule. Many Mexicans wanted independence. Their opposition to Santa Anna had sparked the Texas Revolution in October 1835. Now, Santa Anna led his army into Texas to put down the rebellion.

Santa Anna's troops took San Antonio without

firing a shot. They flew a red flag from a bell tower in the town. It was a warning to Travis and the others at the Alamo. The Mexicans would kill all the defenders if they did not surrender.

Travis responded by firing a single cannonball from the Alamo's largest gun. His message to Santa Anna was clear: The Texians would fight to the end. The Battle of the Alamo had begun.

The bell from San Antonio's tower is now in the Alamo museum.

7

AMERICANS IN TEXAS

The first large group of American settlers had reached Texas years before the Battle of the Alamo. In 1820, Texas was part of Mexico, and Mexico belonged to Spain. That year, Spanish officials gave a miner from Missouri named Moses Austin

Moses Austin

permission to start an American **colony** in Texas. Sadly, Austin died before he could start his colony. The rights to his land passed to his son, Stephen.

In 1821, the younger Austin led 300 American families to land along the Brazos River in southeast Texas. Hundreds more families later settled on Austin's lands. He considered himself

8

San Antonio in the nineteenth century

a loyal Mexican citizen, and he welcomed hard working families who would obey the laws of their new country.

When Austin was preparing to come to Texas, Mexico was winning its independence from Spain. In 1824, Mexico adopted a government similar to the one in the United States. A **constitution** spelled out Mexico's basic laws, and the country was divided into states. Texas was united with the province of Coahuila to form the state of *Coahuila y Texas*.

Stephen Austin brought Americans to Texas in 1821.

The leaders of Coahuila y Texas made it easy for Americans to settle there. By 1830, Texas had about 16,000 Texians, greatly outnumbering the Tejanos. That April, the Mexican government decided to cut off the flow of American settlers by changing Mexico's **immigration** laws. But Americans kept coming to Texas.

Later in 1830, the Mexican government changed another policy affecting the Texians. It began collecting **customs duties**. Under an earlier agreement, the Texians did not have to pay this tax. And they did not want to start paying it now! Tensions increased between the Mexican government and the Texians.

FIRST CONFLICTS

In 1832, trouble broke out in the town of Anahuac. Colonel John Bradburn led the Mexican troops. He was an American working for the Mexican government. William Travis, a lawyer, had just arrived in Anahuac. He soon clashed with Bradburn.

Travis represented a Louisiana man looking for runaway slaves who had escaped to Texas. Bradburn had freed the slaves because slavery was illegal in Mexico. Travis tried to fool Bradburn into turning over the escaped slaves. The trick upset Bradburn and he arrested Travis.

An angry group of Texians demanded Travis's release. These people, like Travis, were angry about the Mexican government's new tax laws. The Texians and Mexicans fought a few

11

William Travis clashes with Colonel John Bradburn and other Mexican officials.

minor gun battles. The incident at Anahuac also led to fighting in Velasco and Nacogdoches.

Finally, Bradburn's commanding officer took over and released Travis. The Mexican commander feared he would lose if the Texians attacked.

The conflicts of 1832 upset Texians. They wanted more independence and the end of the 1830 immigration laws. Some people were willing to use violence if necessary. These Texians were sometimes called "War Dogs." Travis became a leader of this group.

Stephen Austin led its opponents. Austin hoped to use peaceful, political means to make changes in Texas.

Representatives from Texas met in September 1832 and April 1833 to discuss their future. They wrote out a list of demands. They wanted the Mexican government to stop collecting customs duties and allow open immigration again. They also wanted Texas to become a state on its own within Mexico.

At the time of the 1833 meeting, Santa Anna took control of Mexico. Many Texians thought they could get along with Santa Anna. Like them, he had opposed the former Mexican government.

Santa Anna takes control of Mexico.

That government had tried to ignore Mexico's constitution. But the Texians soon learned they could not trust the country's new leader either.

14

ROAD TO REVOLUTION

In November 1833, Austin met with Santa Anna to present the Texians' demands. Santa Anna rejected the request for Texas statehood, but he supported the other demands. Satisfied for now, Austin left Mexico City, the capital, and set out for Texas. He never made it.

In January 1834, the Mexicans arrested him for **treason**. Mexican officials had intercepted a letter Austin had written to Tejano leaders in San Antonio. The letter asked them to seek statehood for Texas, even though Santa Anna opposed it. Austin spent the next year in jail. Afterward, he was forced to remain near Mexico City. He finally returned to Texas in September 1835.

Austin soon discovered that the tensions

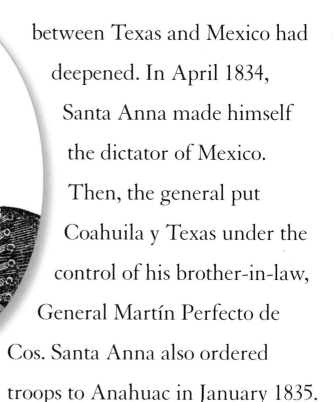

General Martín Perfecto de Cos

between Texas and Mexico had deepened. In April 1834, Santa Anna made himself the dictator of Mexico. Then, the general put Coahuila y Texas under the control of his brother-in-law, General Martín Perfecto de Cos. Santa Anna also ordered troops to Anahuac in January 1835.

Trouble soon erupted in Anahuac. A new tax collector was ordered to collect the customs duties. Texian anger erupted, and Cos sent two messages to the military commander at Anahuac. One message was to be read publicly. This message tried to calm the Texians. The second was a secret message telling the commander that more

16

Mexican troops supporting General Cos

Mexican troops were on the way. Cos assured the commander that "the affairs of Texas will definitely be settled."

Unfortunately for Cos, the second message fell into Texian hands. Travis gathered some volunteer soldiers and took over the Mexican military post at Anahuac. At first, public opinion in Texas opposed this bold move. But when Cos ordered Travis's arrest, the Texians backed Travis. Many now prepared for war.

This was the situation when Austin finally returned home. He, too, was now ready for war. "There is no other remedy," he said, "but to defend our rights, our country, and ourselves by force of arms." The struggle for Texas independence from Mexico was about to begin.

ON THE BATTLEFIELD

On the Mexican side, Cos was also preparing for conflict. He led about 500 troops to San Antonio. In the meantime, the commander at San Antonio began to carry out a new order—take away the Texians' weapons. On September 30, about 100 Mexican troops went to the town of Gonzales to

Cos hoped to capture a cannon much like this one.

19

capture a small cannon. The citizens knew the troops were coming and prepared to resist. On October 2, the Texians fired their cannon and exchanged shots with the Mexicans. The Texas Revolution had officially begun.

A week later, Texian volunteers took over a fort in Goliad, about 95 miles (152 kilometers) southeast of San Antonio. The troops captured rifles and **ammunition**. As October went on, Juan Seguín joined the revolution leading Tejano volunteers. Volunteers from the United States also aided the Texians. The growing army and early victories boosted morale. The Texians marched toward San Antonio, where Cos now had between 750 and 1,000 troops.

Cos sent out patrols to watch for the Texians. Late in October, one of these patrols ran into

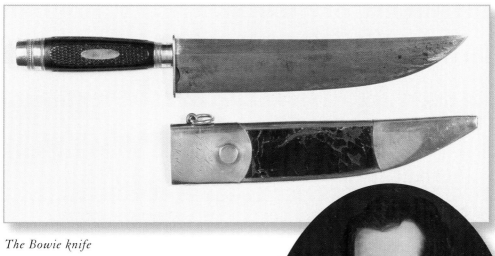

The Bowie knife

Colonel James Bowie and his soldiers. The colonel was famous for his "Bowie knife" and his skills as a knife fighter. Bowie and his men fought off the Mexican patrol. Colonel Bowie also played a major role in another victory against Mexican forces outside San Antonio.

Colonel James Bowie

21

The Alamo today

The Texians were now ready to begin a siege of San Antonio. In a siege, an army surrounds a fort or city held by the enemy. The army hopes to prevent the enemy from receiving supplies or sending messages. The goal is to force the enemy to surrender or to weaken them before an attack.

The Alamo in the nineteenth century

In San Antonio, Cos set up cannons and strengthened his defenses. One of the key spots was the Alamo. Parts of the fort had been built in 1724, with other buildings added later.

At first, the Alamo was a **mission** called *San Antonio de Valero*. Here, Spanish priests lived and

23

Sam Houston

taught Native Americans about the Roman Catholic religion. The mission closed in the 1790s and soon after was turned into a fort. It was named Alamo after the hometown of Mexican soldiers who were stationed there.

The siege of San Antonio lasted for weeks. Little happened on the battlefield. But away from San Antonio, political changes were taking place.

In November, Texian leaders met in San Felipe to discuss the future of Texas. They set up a new government and made Sam Houston commander in chief of the army. He wanted to recruit professional soldiers to fight the Mexicans.

In the meantime, Austin traveled to Washington, D.C. seeking aid for Texas.

On December 5, the Texians finally attacked San Antonio. Soldiers stormed the city as Texian **artillery** fired at the Alamo. For the next several days, the Texians fought to take the city one building at a time. The Mexicans outnumbered the Texians three to one, but the Texians had better rifles and superior shooting skills. They finally took San Antonio.

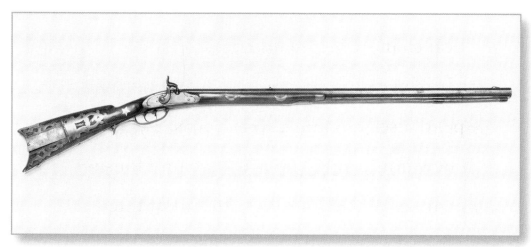

This rifle was used at the Alamo.

WINTER AT THE ALAMO

After the victory in San Antonio, many of the volunteers went home. Only a small force of about 100 soldiers remained, under the command of Colonel James C. Neill. The Texians were running out of food, horses, and other supplies. Many of the men lacked proper clothing for the coming winter.

In mid-January, Neill wrote a letter to Sam Houston. He told Houston that without more troops and supplies, "we must become an easy prey to the enemy, in case of an attack." However, using captured Mexican cannons, Neill and his men turned the Alamo into a strong military fort.

About this time, Houston sent Bowie and some troops to San Antonio. Houston did not think the Alamo could be defended. He instructed

Bowie to blow up the Alamo and move the Texians out of town. But Neill convinced Bowie that the fort was a valuable military post. On February 2, 1836, Bowie wrote to Henry Smith, the governor of Texas. Bowie said he and

Henry Smith

Neill would rather "die in these ditches" than give up the Alamo. Smith agreed to give the fort more arms and troops.

Some reinforcements were already on their way. William Travis, now a colonel in the Texas army, arrived with about thirty soldiers. He was followed by a small group of volunteers led by Davy Crockett.

Davy Crockett

Besides being a skilled soldier and frontiersman from Tennessee, Crockett was also a politician. He had served in the U.S. Congress and even considered running for president. A popular book about Crockett's adventures on the American frontier had made him famous. Now his presence boosted spirits at the fort.

Shortly after Crockett arrived, Neill left San Antonio because of illness in his family. The command was then split between Travis and Bowie. Travis took charge of the Texian army and Bowie led the volunteers.

The combined forces continued to prepare for battle. The defenders at the Alamo had heard reports that Santa Anna and his army were nearby. Some did not believe this news. The next day, however, they learned the truth.

29

Defending the Alamo

SIEGE AT THE ALAMO

General Santa Anna reached San Antonio on February 23 with about 1,500 troops, and thousands more were on their way. When Colonel Travis shot a single cannonball at the Mexicans, they fired back a few grenades into the fort.

Santa Anna's troops on the move

Bowie was angry that Travis had fired the cannon without checking with him. Bowie had wanted to try to talk with Santa Anna before fighting. He sent a message to the Mexican leader. Santa Anna replied that he would not talk with "rebellious foreigners" and called for the Texians to surrender.

Another attempt to talk with Santa Anna failed, and again Travis shot off his 18-pound (8-kilogram) cannon. The Mexicans fired back.

Inside the Alamo were about 150 defenders and 30 civilians. Travis sent a message to Goliad, asking Colonel James Fannin to send reinforcements. Fannin had refused an earlier request for help, since he had to fight his own battles with the Mexicans.

On February 24, Travis made another plea, this time to the United States government. He wrote a letter describing the attack by Santa Anna's artillery. "I shall never surrender or retreat," Travis assured the Americans. Then he said, "I call on you in the name of liberty, of patriotism, and of everything dear to the American character to come to our aid with all [speed]."

By now, Travis was in sole command of the Alamo. On the night of February 23, Bowie went to bed with a high fever. He would remain there for weeks.

FREEMEN OF TEXAS
To Arms!!! To Arms!!!!
"Now's the day, & now's the hour."

CAMP OF THE VOLUNTEERS,
Friday Night, 11 o'clock;
October 2, 1835.

Fellow Citizens:—
We have prevailed on our fellow citizen Wm. H. Wharton, Esq. to return and communicate to you the following express, and also to urge as many as can by possibility leave their homes to repair to Gonzales immediately, "armed and equipped for war even to the knife." On the receipt of this intelligence the Volunteers immediately resolved to march to Gonzales to aid their countrymen. We are just now starting which must apologize for the brevity of this communication. We refer you to Mr. Wharton for an explanation of our wishes, opinions and intentions, and also for side

such political information as has come into our hands. If Texas will now act promptly; she will soon be redeemed from that worse than Egyptian bondage which now cramps her resources and retards her prosperity.

D VID RANDON,
WM. J. BRYAND,
J. W. FANNIN, Jr.
F. T. WELLS,
GEO. SUTHERLAND,
B. T. ARCHER,
W. D. C. HALL,
W. H. JACK,
WM. T. AUSTIN,
P. D. MCNEEL.

P. S. An action took place on yesterday at Gonzales, in which the Mexican Commander and several soldiers were slain—no loss on the American side

A plea for troops to help fight against Mexico

Outside the fort, Santa Anna prepared for a siege. He moved in large cannons and more Mexican troops arrived at the fort. His artillery continued to pound the Alamo, although the damage was not major. The Texians usually fired back with their rifles. They wanted to save their ammunition for the big battle still to come.

On February 29, Travis finally got some good news. A group of thirty-three volunteers

The Mexican army pounded the Alamo with cannon fire.

had managed to reach the Alamo. But within a few days, the situation worsened again. Travis learned that Fannin's troops were not coming. They had tried to leave Goliad but transportation problems had forced them to return.

Now, Santa Anna's troops surrounded the fort, and their cannon fire was doing more damage than before. Travis knew that he and his men would most likely die defending the Alamo.

Texas at the time of the Battle of the Alamo

"REMEMBER THE ALAMO!"

On the morning of March 6, Santa Anna was ready for his final assault. Around 5 A.M., about 1,800 Mexican troops stormed the Alamo. Some shouted Santa Anna's name as they charged, and the noise stirred the Alamo's defenders. A Mexican officer reported, "As soon as our troops

The battle scene on the morning of March 6, 1836

were in sight, a shower of **grapeshot** and musket balls were fired upon them from the fort."

The Mexicans who reached the fort put ladders up against the walls, so that the troops could scurry up and get inside. Travis greeted some of the attackers with a blast from his shot-gun. A moment later, he was dead, killed by a musket shot. Bowie, still sick, was killed in his bed. All around the fort, the defenders fought bravely, but it was useless. The Mexicans had too many men and too many guns.

The Mexicans captured the Texians' prized 18-pound (8-kg) gun and turned it against the other cannons in the fort. The defenders pulled back to a building called the Long Barracks. Now the soldiers were fighting hand to hand. They jabbed with bayonets or clubbed the enemy with

James Bowie was killed in his sickbed.

empty pistols. One Mexican soldier said shouts
of the Texians "pierced our ears with desperate,
terrible cries of alarm in a language we could
not understand."

Within ninety minutes, the fighting was over.
About 190 defenders died, though some historians
say the number was closer to 250. A small group of
men, about five or six, were taken out of the fort
alive. They were then executed under Santa Anna's

orders. Davy Crockett is thought to have been part of this group. A Mexican soldier said, "These unfortunates died without complaining and without humiliating themselves before their torturers." Santa Anna let one slave and the civilians leave the fort alive.

Although he won the Battle of the Alamo, Santa Anna was not finished with the Texians. During the Alamo siege, Texian leaders had

The fall of the Alamo

formally declared their independence. The Mexicans still had a rebellion to crush. They soon won another major victory, at Goliad. Texian commander Sam Houston then retreated with his remaining troops. He waited for just the right time to fight Santa Anna.

That day came on April 21, 1836. Santa Anna had pursued Houston across Texas. Now the two sides met at San Jacinto. Before the battle, Houston

The Battle of San Jacinto

stirred his men's emotions, crying, "Remember the Alamo!" The Texian troops once again fought bravely, and this time they defeated the Mexicans. Houston's victory gave Texas its independence from Mexico.

Today, Texans and other Americans still remember the Alamo. The remains of the fort are a shrine to the Texians, Tejanos, and Americans who died there defending freedom and liberty.

Sam Houston at the battle of San Jacinto.

41

GLOSSARY

ammunition—bullets or shells for guns

artillery—large guns, such as cannons

colony—land under the control of another country

constitution—a document describing the government and basic laws of a country

customs duties—taxes on goods brought into a country

dictator—someone who takes total control of a country

grapeshot—clusters of small iron balls shot from a cannon

immigration—moving to another country to live

mission—a place where people live and teach their religious beliefs

treason—an action meant to betray one's government

DID YOU KNOW?

- In May 1836, Mexican forces knocked down some of the walls of the Alamo so that the Texians could never use it again as a fort.

- During the Civil War (1861–1865), forces from the South occupied the Alamo.

- During the 1870s and 1880s, a Texas merchant owned the Alamo and built a restaurant and saloon there.

- Today, men who visit the Alamo must remove their hats to show respect for its brave defenders.

- Austin, Texas, was named after Stephen Austin, the leader of the Texas colony.

IMPORTANT DATES

Timeline

1821	Stephen Austin brings first American settlers to the Texas colony.
1824	Independent Mexico adopts a constitution; Texas is part of Mexico.
1830	Mexico limits immigration into Texas.
1832	Fighting between Texians and Mexican soldiers in Anahuac.
1833	On April 1, Antonio López de Santa Anna becomes president of Mexico, and Texians call for statehood.
1835	Austin returns to Texas in September; the Texas Revolution begins on October 2; Texian rebels attack San Antonio on October 5 and take the city on October 9.
1836	Santa Anna and his army reach San Antonio on February 23; Mexican forces take the Alamo on March 6; Sam Houston leads the Texians to victory at San Jacinto on April 21, giving Texas its independence.

IMPORTANT PEOPLE

STEPHEN AUSTIN
(1793–1836), *leader of the Texas colony*

JAMES BOWIE
(1796–1836), *colonel in charge of the volunteers at the Alamo*

MARTÍN PERFECTO DE COS
(1800–1854), *Mexican general*

DAVY CROCKETT
(1786–1836), *legendary sharpshooter and volunteer at the Alamo*

SAM HOUSTON
(1793–1863), *commander in chief of the Texian army*

ANTONIO LOPEZ DE SANTA ANNA
(1794–1876), *ruler of Mexico*

JUAN SEGUÍN
(1806–1890), *commander of the Tejano volunteers during the
Texas Revolution*

WILLIAM TRAVIS
(1809–1836), *colonel in charge of Texian troops at the Alamo*

WANT TO KNOW MORE?

At the Library

Carter, Alden R. *Last Stand at the Alamo.* New York: Franklin Watts, 1990.

Hoyt, Edwin P. *The Alamo: An Illustrated History.* Dallas: Taylor Publishing, 1999.

Sullivan, George. *Alamo!* New York: Scholastic, 1997.

On the Web

The Alamo

http://www.thealamo.org

For the official web site for the Alamo

Alamo de Parras

http://www.alamo-de-parras.welkin.org

For a history of the Alamo and the Texas Revolution

Handbook of Texas Online

http://www.tsha.utexas.edu/handbook/online/

For information about the key events leading up to the Battle of the Alamo and the people who took part

Through the Mail

Texas Historical Commission

P.O. Box 12776

Austin, TX 78711

To get information about the Alamo

On the Road

The Alamo National Historic Landmark

300 Alamo Plaza

San Antonio, TX 78299

210/225-1391

To see the Alamo and its museum and library

INDEX

About the Author

Michael Burgan is a freelance writer for children and adults. A history graduate of the University of Connecticut, he has written more than thirty fiction and nonfiction children's books for various publishers. For adult audiences, he has written news articles, essays, and plays. Michael Burgan is a recipient of an Edpress Award and belongs to the Society of Children's Book Writers and Illustrators.